Gaslighting Recovery

A Conscious Guide to Entering the Narcissist's Mind, Overcome the Gaslighting Damage, and Take Control of Your Life

Kevin Delaney

Table of Contents

Introduction 6

Chapter 1: What Is Gaslighting? 7

Common Gaslighting Techniques That You Need to be Aware Of 8

Signs of Gaslighting 10

   Denial 10

   White Lies 11

   Manipulation... 11

   Repetitive Behavior 12

   They Never Apologize 12

   Emotional Projection 13

   Constant Self-Doubt...13

   It Will Wear You Down 13

Chapter 2: How Does Gaslighting Look Like in Different Settings? 15

   Gaslighting in the Family 15

   Gaslighting At Work 17

   Gaslighting in a Romantic Relationship 20

Chapter 3: How Can Gaslighting Affect You? 24

   Loss of Memory 24

   A Constant Feeling of Guilt 24

   Self-Doubt...25

   Anxiety 26

   Loss of Self-Esteem... 26

   Depression 27

Chapter 4: Tips to Disarm a Gaslighter................................29

   Step 1 – Recognize the Signs 29

   Step 2 – Keep a Log of Events 30

    Step 3 – Minimize Direct Contact 30

   Step 4 – Prioritize Self-Esteem 31

   Step 5 – Set Healthy Boundaries.....................................33

   Step 6 – Seek Help From Friends and Family 34

Chapter 5: Recovery Phase 1 – Practicing Acknowledgment and Self-Compassion......................**36**

Acknowledge the Abuse....................................37

Practicing Self-Compassion.............................. 39

Indulge in Forgiveness.................................. 40

Practice 3rd Person Self-Talk........................41

Increase Your Desire for Self Preservation................41

Strive to Bring About a Change 42

Take a Proactive Approach to Get Rid of Negative Self-Talk.. 42

Be Mindful.. 43

Chapter 6: Recovery Phase 2 – Work on Your Self-Esteem.......................... **44**

How Can One's Self-Esteem be Affected When Gaslighted?.......45

How to Regain One's Self-Esteem? 46

Chapter 7: Recovery Phase 3 – Build Healthy Boundaries..........................**52**

Here's How Gaslighting Violates Your Boundaries 52

Lying...52

Labeling Hurtful Comments As a Joke.....................53

Changing Expectations Suddenly Claiming That They Were the Same Since the Beginning.................................54

Accusing You Vaguely That You Have Not Been Able to Keep Up With the Expectations...................................54

Making You Feel Responsible For Their Actions, Thoughts, and Feelings 55

Expecting You to Portray Them As a Very Good Person in Public..56

They Will Publicly Shame You.............................56

How to Set Boundaries to Protect Yourself? 57

Name Your Feelings and Limits 57

Be Assertive...57

Permit Yourself to Set Boundaries 58

Remember that Boundaries Can be Flexible.................59

Chapter 8: A Step-by-Step Approach to Heal From Emotional and Psychological Abuse 60

Step 1 – Acknowledge What Happened to You 60

Step 2 – Change Your Negative Thinking Patterns 61

Step 3 – Practice Self-Care 63

Step 4 – Allow Others to Support You 64

Chapter 9: Writing Exercises That Will Help in Healing 66

Can Writing Help to Heal? 67

Some Writing Prompts That Can Be Helpful 69

Chapter 10: Protecting Yourself Against Manipulators in Everyday Life 72

Stop Falling Into Their Traps 72

Start Noting Down Everything They Say While Conversing With You 72

Try Steering Clear Whenever It is Possible 73

Try Keeping a Backup 73

Start Calling Them Out on Their Behavior 74

Don't Get Emotionally Attached to Them 74

Try Meditating Often 75

Try Inspiring Them 75

Try Not to Get Too Empathetic 76

Start Telling Them That They Are Right 76

Try Letting Go of the Harmful Relationships 77

Develop a Strong Mentality 77

Practice Positive Self-Talk 78

Conclusion 79

Introduction

Congratulations on purchasing *Gaslighting Recovery*, and thank you for doing so.

The following chapters will discuss what gaslighting is, how it is so common in today's relationships, and how you can come out from the clutches of a gaslighter.

In very simple words, gaslighting is a term that refers to a type of emotional manipulation where the main aim of the abuser is to make you question your sanity. This gives the abuser the upper hand in the relationship, and they can make you do whatever they want to fulfill their ulterior motives. Contrary to what most people think, gaslighting is not only seen in personal or romantic relationships but is also very common in professional setups. With time, the victims start doubting themselves, and they become very sure of the fact that something is gravely wrong with them.

My aim in this book is to create a general awareness about gaslighting because that is the first thing you need to protect yourself from the gaslighters around you. The moment you learn to recognize it, you can arm yourself with strategies that will protect you. When the gaslighter is someone very close to you or someone you trust, it becomes even more challenging to identify the signs of gaslighting, but in this book, I have explained how you can do so.

Even if you have been a victim of gaslighting for years, healing is possible, and we will discuss that in this book. The chapters will reveal several steps that you can take to return to your normal life and free yourself from the toxic relationship with the gaslighter.

There are plenty of books on this subject on the market, thanks again for choosing this one! Every effort was made to ensure it is full of as much useful information as possible. Please enjoy!

Chapter 1: What Is Gaslighting?

At its very core, gaslighting is a tactic of abuse. The abuser uses it with the aim of gaining the upper hand on the victim to the point that the victim is no longer sure about his/her own reality and starts questioning it. It is a very slow process – the abuser spins his web taking his sweet time, and this itself makes it difficult to spot gaslighting in the first instance. In extreme cases, the victim might even start to question whether they remember things correctly or whether their reaction to some event is more than necessary. And when the victim has reached this stage, the abuser will then start making them understand that whatever they say is the only 'truth.'

The origin of the term 'gaslighting' goes way back to 1938, and you'd be surprised to know where this word was used for the first time – it was actually in a play! The name of the play was 'Gas Light.' The story of the play goes something like this – the husband manipulates the wife into believing that she is not mentally sound. He starts making several changes in their house and the wife's surroundings, one of which was that he reduced the intensity of the gaslights. After that, he told his wife that this is not happening in reality and that she imagines it. In the story, the goal of the husband was to prove that his wife is mentally unstable so that he can take her inheritance after admitting her to an asylum.

Gaslighting starts in a very subtle way that you often overlook. For example, let us say someone is narrating an incident. If the abuser listens to the narration, he might ask questions about very small details and challenge them. These details might not even be significant. Now, the person narrating the story might, at that point, admit that yes, they were wrong, but they will move on. But the abuser will not leave it as it is. He will keep using that single victory in the future to discredit the victim's other narrations. Slowly, they will start questioning whether the victim's memory is reliable enough.

At first, the victim might fight back, saying that they know what they are doing or saying. Their intuition might even suggest that things are not how they should be and that something is fishy. They might think that their relationship is growing toxic. But every incident of gaslighting is so subtle that the victim is never able to find out what it is that is actually making them feel uneasy in the relationship. When this continues for a long time, the victim often gives in and starts questioning themselves and second-guesses their memories or emotions. In fact, the victim might even start depending on the abuser to tell them whether they remember things correctly or whether they are reasonable in a particular situation. This formation of trust gives the abuser an added benefit, and they misuse it to its greatest extent. In popular culture, you will often find that it is being shown that only a man is gaslighting his wife or girlfriend. But gaslighting is not gender-specific. It can be done by anyone. And it not only happens in romantic relationships but also in workplaces. We are going to go over that in greater detail in the next chapter.

Common Gaslighting Techniques That You Need to be Aware Of

There are many forms of gaslighting. Sometimes it is done in a very emotional and verbal way. In contrast, at other times, it might be done indirectly and in a very manipulative way. In this section, we are going to go over some common techniques that gaslighters use. Knowing these will make it easier for you to spot the gaslighters in your life.

- **Countering** – The most common method of gaslighting is when the abuser is questioning the victim's memories. They usually do this by completely denying the account of events given by the victim, saying that none of it happened in reality. They might ask the victim directly about whether they are sure of what they are saying since they have such a bad memory. The abuser might even invent things of his own that did not happen in real life just to prove their point and to make the victim feel even more lost.

- **Withholding** – This is when the abuser is refusing to partake in any conversation because they are withholding information. So, the abuser will pretend that they cannot understand a single thing that the victim is saying, or they will simply deny listening to any of their concerns. They will say that they don't have time to listen to them because all they say is nonsense. Or, they might even tell the victim that they are intentionally speaking nonsensical things to confuse the abuser.
- **Denial/Forgetting** – This is a very common technique used by abusers when they want to discredit the victim's version of events. They simply deny the things from having occurred in the first place. They might even say that they had never promised anything; they do this to dodge any form of responsibility. Another form of denial is accusing the victim of making things up and that they did not happen in reality.
- **Trivializing** – This is when the victim is exposed to hurtful behavior, but when they react to it, they are accused of behaving in an exaggerated manner even if their reaction is justified. When a person is consistently exposed to this kind of behavior, they start believing that their own emotions are either excessive or invalid. Suppose they crack a joke and you feel hurt by it. They might tell you that you are too sensitive and that everyone found it funny except you, whereas, in reality, your concerns or your feelings were valid.
- **Diversion/Blocking** – When an abuser uses this technique, they will create a diversion in the actual topic and shift the focus of the discussion to the credibility of the victim. In this way, the attention is shifted from what really needs to be discussed. The abuser might even create a situation where the events are twisted to form an argument about whether the victim can be trusted or not with their account of things. They might blame you for talking to your friends or family members, saying that they are the ones who are always putting the bad thoughts and ideas in your head.
- **Stereotyping** – Lastly, there is another technique that abusers use where the abuser might engage in certain

negative stereotypes to prove their point and manipulate the victim even further. These stereotypes might be related to their nationality, gender, sexuality, ethnicity, race, and so on. A very common example is when a male abuser tells a female victim that she is crazy and irrational to seek therapy or help.

It is true that gaslighting can happen to anyone and anywhere. Still, it is mostly seen in social interactions and intimate relationships where the power balance is not present between two people. So, the gaslighter tries to gain the upper hand.

Signs of Gaslighting

The last thing anyone expects from the people they love is gaslighting, but it happens, and we are often so blinded with love that we fail to notice it. In this section, we will go over some important signs that will help you spot gaslighting right away.

Denial

The first and foremost sign that someone is gaslighting you is when they are constantly engaging in denial. Even if you produce them with sufficient proof that they are lying, they will straightaway deny it. Their main motive behind this is to alter and hamper what you think is the truth. This will, in turn, give rise to doubts in your mind – doubts regarding the proof you have. The abuser will always try to dodge any form of confrontation with you. Their best weapon is denial so that they can easily flip back and not keep their promise. Another sign that comes hand-in-hand with denial is the silent treatment.

You need to keep a close eye on the person you suspect of gaslighting you. Confront them with whatever you have in mind? Do they answer respectfully and understand their mistakes? Or, are they trying to deny everything you said to them? Did they explicitly say that they are not going to badmouth you to the boss and went and did the same anyway and, when confronted, denied the whole thing? Well, yes, then you are a victim of gaslighting. This is a clear sign!

Let me give you another example to show you how denial works – suppose you told your spouse to take out the trash before leaving for work, and he tells you that he will. He then leaves for work without doing the chore. When you later find out about this, you dispose of the trash yourself. Later, when your spouse comes back home, you tell him that he forgot to take the trash out, and so you did it. But he denies that and says that it was him who disposed of the garbage and not you. You keep opposing him, and he keeps insisting on his version of the truth. When things like this keep happening, you feel confused and start questioning whether you really forget stuff.

White Lies

Another common sign of gaslighting is when someone is feeding you with white lies. The abuser might impose the lie on you and then blame you for inaccuracy and confusion. Whatever the gaslighter says to you will never be at par with their actions. For example, let us say that your girlfriend tells you that your favorite movie is *The Breakfast Club,* but you deny and say that no, it is *Gladiator*; she might say that you repeatedly told her in the past that it's *The Breakfast Club* then this is a white lie that she is using to confuse and gaslight you. Her adamant behavior will force you to believe that maybe you did tell her in the past and forgot, and maybe you have started to forget small details of reality, and thus, your memory cannot be trusted.

Manipulation

The abuser will use gaslighting techniques to twist things their way and manipulate you into doing or believing stuff that you don't want to. They do this so that you start depending on them even more, and thus, they can completely eliminate the competition for your love. They will use several manipulatory techniques to get things done their way so that, ultimately, all their needs have been satisfied. And in order to this, they won't care a bit about how you feel, and they won't leave any stone unturned. They will get what they want through any means, and they won't even stop using your loved ones against you.

So, if your boyfriend comes to you with a gift that you wanted for a long time, but they want a favor in return, then it is manipulation, and he might even be doing it to gaslight you. Whatever it is, you need to understand that it is not love!

Another example is when your wife is trying to manipulate and sever your ties with your parents even when she knows how close you are to them. She might use white lies to make you believe that they are not good, and so, you should not trust them. This will poison your heart towards your parents. She might even say things like your mother told her bad things or treated her insultingly, whereas, in reality, these things might not even have happened. A very common move of an abuser is convincing the victim that they are the only ones speaking the truth and that everyone around them is a liar they shouldn't trust.

Repetitive Behavior

Repetitive behaviors such as constant nagging from the other person's side are often a sign of gaslighting, mostly if the nagging is about changing some major things about you that you don't want to change. On the other hand, if you ask the other person to change something, they won't listen to you and keep doing the same thing over and over again. Even if you tell them that you find something unsettling or disturbing and you don't want them to repeat it, they will not listen to you. These are some signs that the person is not engaging in a healthy relationship with you and is primarily showings signs of a gaslighter.

They Never Apologize

Gaslighters never apologize for anything. Even in a romantic relationship, if one of the partners is gaslighting the other and the victim makes it clear to the abuser that he/she is hurt or that they do not like something, the abuser will not apologize and, on top of that, continue doing the same thing without any care. If you are facing this too then, it is a telltale sign that you are in a relationship with a gaslighter. When this thing continues for too long, the victim will simply exhaust themselves because the abuser never takes any responsibility or accountability for anything they do. With time, the victim starts to think that their emotions are completely invalid.

Emotional Projection

Gaslighters, just like any other human being, have their own shortcomings. And when they try to manipulate others through various techniques, they somehow try to project those shortcomings onto others. They do this to create a diversion from the main topic so that no one can find the time to accuse them of everything they have done. So, if someone in your life is constantly projecting their own emotional problems on you and also accusing you of doing things you didn't, then you are a victim of gaslighting. The gaslighter makes this their main tool so that the victim is totally occupied with defending themselves and, in the process, forgets or overlooks what the main topic is and that they are being gaslighted.

Constant Self-Doubt

Everything that the gaslighter does is toxic, but one of the major things that you cannot possibly overlook is pushing the victim onto the very edge where they constantly doubt themselves. This feeling can cripple you to your very core. You will slowly become hesitant before doing even the simplest tasks, and you will keep thinking of what the other person will think or whether you are right with your version of things.

It Will Wear You Down

Do you know why gaslighting is so destructive to mental health? It is because when it is carried on for an extended period of time, it wears down the victim and drains away all their energy. Their perception of reality is changed, and their conscience is also affected. With time, it slowly eats away at their sense of self-confidence, and the victim is no longer sure of anything and often feels confused and lost. They start questioning their own sanity.

All of the signs that I have mentioned above are the major ones that you will notice when you are a victim of gaslighting. There are several other signs as well, like constant negativity or a sense of guilt even though you have done nothing wrong. But all of these signs have one thing in common – they will make you question yourself. You will become convinced that it is you who is wrong and not the other person. That's how gaslighting works, but if you don't want to be a victim to it anymore, read this book and walk on the path of recovery.

Chapter 2: How Does Gaslighting Look Like in Different Settings?

Many people think that gaslighting is only present in romantic or intimate relationships. But it is not limited to that. It is present everywhere, and in this chapter, we are going to explore how gaslighting looks in different settings.

Gaslighting in the Family

Is there a family member you don't like because they constantly shove you aside and say that your recollection of events is not right? Yes? Then you have a gaslighter in the family. You'd be surprised to know that you are not alone in this. Apparently, gaslighting has become very common in family settings, and it is extremely sad. When gaslighting is present in the family, it often takes a long time for that person to recognize it mostly because we don't usually expect our own family members to do that with us. And even if you do identify it, in most cases, you will still keep questioning whether your memory is serving you right. But listen to me – you are not crazy!

Gaslighting starts with very small events that might not even matter at that point until the abuser starts feeding you with more and more distorted information and your self-confidence takes a hit. Let me give you a very common example. Suppose you grew up in a household where you had a narcissistic mother. She will keep a very high public persona and keep telling everyone how self-sacrificing, caring, and a perfect example of a mother she was. But you don't remember her like that. Whenever she praises herself in front of others, you feel like it never happened because it didn't. And if you try to confront her, reminding her of all those days she left you alone and abused you, she will completely deny it, saying that you don't remember anything, and she might even tell others that you have been a very imaginative child ever since you were a kid. This is a classic case of parental gaslighting. And it is quite easy for you as an adult to think that your version of events is wrong because you were a child then, and you jump to the conclusion that you indeed don't remember things correctly. This is where your mother plants that first seed of doubt in your mind.

After this, the lies keep increasing and getting bigger. They are no longer insignificant. And before you realize it, you are deep into the web of the gaslighter, and you can't separate what's right and what's wrong because you no longer have faith in your own decisions and memories.

Some common gaslighting language in the family includes – 'You are too sensitive at all times,' 'This is not what happened; you are exaggerating the events,' 'I never said anything like that,' and so on. They might even impose things on you by saying 'you said...' when you never said anything remotely close to what the family said you did. They make generalized statements such as 'Everyone believes you are...' so that the victim starts feeling they are alone in this and that everyone excluding them is thinking the same. Another common way of gaslighting is when they try to impose guilt on you and make you feel sorry for things you didn't do, and the most common sentence they use is 'I only did what I did because...'

Gaslighting can happen at any moment, but the most common instance is when you are trying to confront one of your family members regarding something that's questionable of them, or they are inconsistent with everything they do. At its very core, gaslighting is nothing but trying to dodge the actual problem and present the audience with a 'cover-up' situation. The gaslighter will try to confuse everyone else around them so that no one knows what really happened and the details are all muddled up.

Another very common way in which gaslighting is used as a weapon in toxic families is to justify their abusive behavior. For example, women often have to face so many injustices at their in-laws – they are abused in several ways. But often, these behaviors of the in-laws are justified by the entire family by giving several excuses, the most common of which is 'none of it is personal.' In fact, many a time, the woman's reaction is thought to be exaggerated and questioned extensively by everyone.

In a family setting, when things are too conservative or strict, there might be someone challenging the ways. In that case, family members resort to gaslighting because it serves to be a powerful weapon to prevent any form of change. For example, if the child of the family wants to pursue a different career option than what the parents are asking him to, the parents might often question his abilities in his chosen path to make him doubtful of his abilities. And if the child becomes upset or sad because he is not allowed to pursue the career of his choice, he will be passed along to be overly sensitive.

For people who have been in such families for years, identifying gaslighting is not easy. Sometimes people can only identify that they are being gaslighted when they get to spend some time with a healthy family, and they get their reality check. So, some strong signs of gaslighting in the family are when your decisions are never cared for, any questions or changes are met with passive-aggressiveness, ridicule, or worse – denial.

Gaslighting At Work

Gaslighting in the workplace is quite common, and it is usually committed by those who can abuse the power that is vested upon them by the company. Or, it can also be done by someone in the office who is liked by most people and thus, he/she thinks that they have some kind of upper hand on others. All of these people are what we know as toxic coworkers. Thus, it can be a disgruntled client, a prejudiced workgroup, a scheming coworker, or a negative manager. Gaslighting at the workplace is not only done towards individuals but also towards groups.

One of the most common examples of gaslighting that is commonly seen at work is sabotaging. Let's say that you have worked very hard on a presentation for an important client. At the time of submission, since your coworker is already meeting with the boss, he is asked to turn in your presentation as well. But later that day, the boss calls you to his office and asks you for an update on the presentation because you haven't submitted it yet. You then tell him that it was completed on due time and your coworker was supposed to submit it. At the same time, your coworker is spying on your conversation and barges in, saying that you shouldn't blame others for the work that you have not done on time. This is a very common example of workplace sabotage.

The main thing with saboteurs is that they never want you to succeed. This is a sick mentality, but they think that your failure would somehow make them look good in the eyes of your superiors. But what they fail to realize is that when someone fails at the office, it brings a bad name to the entire company as a whole, and this includes the saboteur too. However, in order to fulfill their goals, they will go to any length and even lie straightaway to your face. Another common thing that you will notice in the gaslighters at the office is that they often blame others for things that they are doing – this is a classic case of projection, and it is very frequently seen.

The gaslighter will place false accusations against you that will put your credibility and performance into question. They spread such a form of negativity around the office, and this is mostly based on biased accusations and personal judgment but not any solid facts. They will show passive-aggressiveness towards you in the form of negative gossip. They might even spread rumors either about your personal life or professional qualification to taint your image.

The negative smearing of your image might even continue beyond the arena of simple gossip. The gaslighter might make public comments about you at meetings or even face-to-face to intimidate you and break your self-confidence. But again, these negative accusations will never have any validity to them. They are mostly based on exaggerations and falsehoods. The gaslighters at work might even marginalize or belittle you by throwing leud and accusatory comments hidden under humor or sarcasm. In this way, they easily get away even after expressing a condescending and hostile attitude towards coworkers. They often use the term 'just kidding' right after they tease you or mock you. Even when you are capable professionally of being included in certain things, they will deliberately exclude you from these. This can include promotions, meetings, leadership opportunities, or any other form of professional development. And the gaslighters won't even give you any reasonable justification for their behavior. They will do it just because they want to. Intimidation at the workplace by a gaslighter is not only done by these means, but they can also bully you quite visibly.

So, ask yourself – are you constantly doubting your decisions or second-guessing yourself? Is there someone at work – maybe your superior or a coworker – who is constantly countering everything you say? These are signs that you are being gaslighted. The most common effect of gaslighting at work is that the victim feels confused and doesn't know what to do. This lack of self-confidence gives the gaslighter further more opportunity to make you their target – they get the upper hand, and they will make you feel that they are always correct. They might throw back-handed compliments at you, and you will feel guilty and hurt even after doing the job far better than others.

When this same thing keeps happening for a long time, you start questioning your self-worth. The gaslighter will continuously make you feel as if you are not cut out for this job, and thus, you are performing terribly. You will keep feeling hurt, and these feelings, when suppressed, might accumulate and start evading your personal life. In no time, they will start affecting your perceptions of who you are as a person and, when it comes to outside the office environment, whether you are capable of doing anything at all.

That toxic feeling of always being the one with lesser qualities in a team makes you feel the same in life. Your personal self-worth and your credibility as an employee both come into question in your perception. You slowly start wondering that probably the gaslighter's judgments and accusations are not so false, and maybe the fault lies with you. The moment you do this, you fall deeper into their trap and allow them to manipulate you even further.

Gaslighting is nothing but a toxic rewiring of the brain and is very similar to brainwashing.

Gaslighting in a Romantic Relationship

Even in a romantic relationship, there is a fight for power and control. In some cases, this happens quite openly, but in most cases, it happens in a covert manner by using toxic tactics like gaslighting. Why someone is gaslighting their partner differs from one couple to the other. There is no straight answer to this question. Everyone rationalizes their behavior in a different manner. But gaslighting is very common in romantic relationships.

Sometimes, one of the partners thinks that the other person is going to leave them and that they are no longer in love or that their relationship is too fragile. They resort to gaslighting to keep the relationship alive, but it becomes abusive and toxic. In their minds, the gaslighters think that there was no other way to sustain that relationship other than gaslighting. But this is not what happens in all relationships. In some cases, one partner resorts to gaslighting just to feel good and superior. They genuinely feel that gaslighting helps them control their partner and that somehow gives them internal satisfaction. As harsh as it may sound, this happens in reality. They simply derive pleasure and happiness from being able to control the other person.

The impact of gaslighting on the victim and the relationship, in general, is destructive. There are so many forms of gaslighting in relationships. A very common one is to lie and then exaggerate the details. The abuser might produce accusations and false presumptions against the victim and create an imaginary negative narrative with the sole purpose of gaining control by tainting the image of the victim. They might say things like, you are a loser, or you are good for nothing.

And the worst part is that they will keep repeating these false accusations until there comes the point where you actually start believing them. This gives them the chance to dominate the relationship, control every conversation you engage in, and always stay on the offensive.

If you go and challenge them, they will try to quickly escalate all the accusations they have against you. Gaslighters never like being called upon for their mistakes. They will triple down on their toxic techniques and use blame, denial, and what not to refute any evidence or proof you present in front of them. They will constantly try to misdirect the entire conversation so that no one can ever be able to blame them for anything. They will sow the seeds of confusion and doubt so that with time, you no longer believe in your own self. In fact, there have been cases where one partner caught the other sexting with someone else, and when they were confronted about it, they denied it on their face and even said that none of it ever happened. They try to prove that the other partner has a wild imagination and that they are crazy!

Eventually, when the same thing continues for too long, the victim wears down and no longer has the energy or mental capacity to try and prove every point. They become pessimistic and start doubting themselves. They question their own reality and perception and start believing in all those false accusations. The ultimate aim of every gaslighter is to be able to hold the strings to the other person and control them at every point, and that is exactly what happens in romantic relationships as well.

But the most common question in everyone's minds when it comes to romantic settings is why partners become gaslighters in the first place. Well, you cannot see it as a direct form of psychological or emotional abuse because it doesn't happen that way. Gaslighting is mostly seen as a way to resolve conflicts in an easier manner without taking the blame for anything. Thus, the gaslighter tries to neutralize all the accusations by throwing counter-accusations and then justify their own actions with further false and made-up stories. It is mostly laziness to take some active actions and the emotional immaturity of a partner that leads to gaslighting in relationships.

When a gaslighter uses all his toxic tactics to resolve a conflict and suppress the victim, they manage to keep them quiet. They go to bed thinking that they have been fruitful in solving the conflict but is it? With time, the abuser keeps justifying his abusive behavior thinking that they wouldn't have had to resort to such lengths if only their partner had fixed their behavior.

But no one is a born gaslighter – they become one. In most cases, it has been seen that people who gaslight others have faced the same thing at one point or the other in their own life. It might be possible that they have grown up in a dysfunctional family where gaslighting was a usual thing, and that is how they learned it.

In other cases, adults are not even aware of the fact that they are actually gaslighting their partners by doing those things. Sometimes people pick up the habit of gaslighting at such a young age that it becomes a usual thing for them. They find it quite natural to resort to those techniques to get what they want in life. So, in very simple words, they are not even aware of their toxic methods.

Lastly, there's another reason why gaslighting happens in romantic relationships. It is because the abuser wants to feel empowered. They are shy or submissive in real life, and so they always seek partners who they can prey on. Their partners are those people who can be subdued with no extra effort. And when these introvert abusers are able to suppress others, it makes them feel good about themselves.

No matter what type of setting we are talking about, the ultimate motive of every gaslighter is to build a certain amount of dependence on their victims. The gaslighter makes the victim question their own abilities so that they can rely on the gaslighter for every big and small decision of their lives. Thus, in the life of the victim, the gaslighter holds all power. But in order to keep the relationship between them alive, the gaslighter might give the victim a small amount of hope from time to time – just enough to hold on to. But all of that is superficial. The constant exposure to manipulation and all sorts of coercion ultimately breaks the victim and pushes them into an unending pit of insecurity.

23

Chapter 3: How Can Gaslighting Affect You?

Gaslighting can affect you in multiple ways, especially when it's being done to you over a considerable period of time. In this chapter, we are going to see and learn the different long-term effects gaslighting can have on a victim.

Loss of Memory

By now, you all must have understood that when someone is gaslighting you, they are altering your perceptions of reality; it's as if they are overwriting your memory with things that never happened. Over a period of time, it is very natural for every victim to start questioning their every thought, detail, and memory. But most importantly, you are being hurt multiple times. You experience emotional trauma, and this has a direct impact on the hippocampus region of your brain. This region is responsible for forming memories in the human brain, and when you are under stress or a period of prolonged sadness, then the hippocampus starts shrinking, which, in turn, causes memory loss. And this is not only when you are with the gaslighter. Even if you manage to come out of his/her control, emotional abuse often leaves long-term repercussions on the victim in the form of C-PTSD, PTSD, and phobias.

A Constant Feeling of Guilt

Gaslighting and guilt-tripping go hand in hand. One of the major tactics used by gaslighters is guilt. They manipulate you in such a way that you will feel guilty and sorry for having any feelings at all. Like I told you earlier, gaslighting, at its very core, is a tactic used by abusive people to hide their own wrongdoings. Similarly, they will create such a situation that they will blame you for everything that they have done. You will be made the scapegoat in every situation, even when you have done nothing wrong. Guilt is something that can separate you from all the beliefs and convictions you have, and this is what the gaslighter will use against you.

For example, if you have certain expectations from the gaslighter and they were not able to keep up with them or follow through, then they will blame you for it instead of taking accountability. They will say that your expectations were too high and you should be ashamed of yourself even when what you expected from them was very basic. This is how they put the guilt on you, and when guilt is being used like this, there is no escaping such a vicious cycle. And do you know what is gives the gaslighter their advantage? They know that they can make you feel guilty, and you will, in turn, have some sort of obligation to feel that guilt. The only way out of this is not to give in and stick to your convictions. We will discuss how you can deal with a gaslighter in the latter part of this book.

Self-Doubt

One of the most widespread effects of gaslighting is that it makes people doubt themselves after a certain point in time. That is how gaslighters gain the upper hand on you – they make you doubt your own perception and reality. Since the gaslighters trick you into believing that your account of events did not happen or they are not valid, you slowly start doubting everything about yourself. Self-doubt can be paralyzing, and it can even hamper the process of healing. It can delay your recovery even after you have come out of the clutches of the gaslighter. You doubt your traumatic memories, too, and so, it is very easy for the victim to go into denial instead of dealing with those horrors. Denial, then, becomes an automatic response for such victims. In fact, there are instances where the victim started doubting their diagnosis too because they have been repeatedly told that they imagine things, and so they think that maybe this time they are making this up in their minds.

It's not so easy to fix or reverse the effects of such an extended period of gaslighting, but it's not completely impossible at the same time. After a few months of gaslighting, self-doubt can adversely affect your mind and even push you to the brink of depression. You always have this lingering feeling of incompetence in life that will make you feel that you are good for nothing. All of this leads to chronic fatigue. Your self-will is affected, and so is your self-esteem.

Anxiety

Since you are always on the verge of doubting yourself and your decisions, it is very natural for the victims of gaslighting to also feel anxious. You lose your hold on reality and start losing your sanity after a certain point, and this causes anxiety attacks in several people. Some people even start having nightmares because of the emotional trauma they are carrying. Their feelings have been ignored and invalidated for so long that they themselves now doubt their existence. There are others who also develop suicidal ideation.

All the manipulation that a victim is subjected to at the hands of the gaslighter completely impairs their own emotions. In fact, experts say that some victims of gaslighting also show symptoms of obsessive-compulsive disorder. They develop this from the fact that the gaslighter has forced them to constantly re-check themselves, and this went on for a considerable period of time before they developed OCD.

Loss of Self-Esteem

Whether the gaslighting abused you intentionally or unintentionally, your self-esteem will take a direct hit, and you will increasingly feel disempowered. This happens because the abuser takes away your right to speak up. You are never allowed to speak up about your feelings or ask for what you need. And when the victim gathers up the courage to speak up, the abuser might use their words against them or shut them up using some other covert tactic. With time, the victim becomes even more submissive and realizes that life is easier if they listen to the abuser and remain quiet. But in order to feel human, everyone must have their voice – gaslighting forces you to shut that voice down, and so, you have no other option than to feel powerless.

Moreover, a gaslighter will constantly make you feel as if you are nothing and no one. When the victim is ridiculed to such an extent, after some time, they no longer remember who they are. For example, if your boyfriend is a gaslighter and he makes fun of your hobbies, the girlfriend often finds it easier to keep the hobby aside than to stand against the gaslighter because it's mostly futile. Somewhere along with all those nasty comments and criticism of the victim, the person loses themselves. They start doing everything according to the preferences of the gaslighter.

Not every gaslighter will do things under the sun. Some of them will manipulate or put down the victim in a subtler way. And this is why even victims fail to notice the injustice that they are being subjected to. The victim might be withstanding a lot of manipulation, and their self-esteem is battered. Just because it is being done by a person close to them, they don't notice it until it's too late, until their sense of self is completely destroyed.

Depression

Several gaslighting victims fall prey to depression because the abusers do not stop until they reach the very core of that person and destroy them from within. They completely rewire your thinking process and make you dependent on them. You start questioning your reactions and even your feelings just because the gaslighter told you that you are neurotic or you are behaving in an exaggerated manner.

People who are on the receiving end of such abusive behavior usually cannot pinpoint exactly where things have gone wrong. Similarly, you might not even be able to say that you are depressed. These things have to be identified clinically, but you can definitely understand that someone is gaslighting you by following the signs mentioned in Chapter 1.

Even if you try to discuss your feelings and grievances with the gaslighter, they will try to change the subject or blame you for everything that's happening. They will downplay you by constantly making you feel that your emotions are inconsequential. But the worst thing is that they will also shower you with some small gestures of love from time to time so that you cling on to the hope that they have changed. They do it only to keep you in their trap. And such sudden changes in emotions leave the victim even more confused. It is important for you to take some stand against gaslighting and not keep compromising for mistakes that you never committed. I hope this chapter has opened your eyes to the destructive effects gaslighting can have on you. If you are confused as to how you can stand up for yourself, don't worry, I will cover it in a step-by-step manner in the next chapter.

Chapter 4: Tips to Disarm a Gaslighter

Before I tell you the different measures you can take to disarm a gaslighter, I want you to understand that gaslighting is not a form of love. It's about control and power, but when the gaslighting is being done by someone close to you, it's very natural for you to mistake it for love and concern. However, those people are not your well-wishers. They have their own agendas, and they are gaslighting you to fulfill those agendas. If you follow the steps mentioned in this chapter, you can step out of this malicious cycle. It might not be so easy as it sounds but with persistence, you'll be able to do it

Step 1 – Recognize the Signs

The first step is obviously to recognize the fact that you are being gaslighted by someone. If you don't realize that you have become the victim of gaslighting, it won't be possible for you to carry on with the next steps. Always remember that gaslighting does not happen overnight. It starts in a subtle way but carries on for a long time. Your abuser will keep manipulating and tricking you into doubting your reality. And by the time he's done with you, you will feel lost and confused. It becomes difficult for the victim to understand how they reached that stage in life. But that is why I made a separate chapter in this book, pinpointing the signs that you should look out for – once you have that awareness, identifying the signs becomes a whole lot easier.

Moreover, did you know that it becomes easier for the gaslighter to manipulate you into doing everything his way when you are not aware of things? This is because ignorance itself takes away your power. But when you know everything or at least try to understand what's going on, you are far better equipped to tackle the situation. When you are aware of the fact that you are being gaslighted, the abuser might even consider changing their prime target because they don't want to be exposed to society for what they are. The knowledge of the fact that you are being gaslighted will also give you more confidence and throw the abuser off their game. So, educating yourself is the first step.

Step 2 – Keep a Log of Events

The gaslighter will try to discredit whatever you say in order to prove to the world that you are not reliable. So, in order to disarm a gaslighter, it is often advised that you should maintain your own log of events and conversations. This will help you not lose touch with your own sanity. If someone constantly keeps telling you that you imagine stuff over the long term, it is very easy to believe all that and start questioning their own reality. That is exactly what happens in gaslighting. So, when you maintain a journal or keep a note of the exact conversations and events, you know that you are not wrong in your perception of things and that the abuser is just trying to gaslight you.

When you see your recollection of events every time the abuser denies your accusations, you can remind yourself that no, you are right, and he is wrong. I understand that it is very difficult coming to terms with the fact that you are being gaslighted, especially when that person is someone close to you. But even if the person gaslighting you is your go-to, you need to take a step back and talk to someone trustable about this toxic behavior. At that time, this log of events will prevent you from second-guessing yourself.

If the gaslighting is happening to you at work, then there is another way in which you can keep a log – you can copy your team members in emails whenever you can. Always try to incorporate written documentation wherever it is possible to do so. If you are having a meeting, make sure you have someone else to vouch for it. Questioning your sanity will be much harder for anyone when you have solid proof of interactions and witnesses.

Step 3 – Minimize Direct Contact

Since gaslighters try their best to distort your reality into something that works for them, it is better that you minimize your direct contact with them. In most situations, people often keep to themselves even if they suspect that they are being gaslighted. But that is a mistake. If you think that the more people you involve, the more dram you are inviting, that's not the case while interacting with a gaslighter. But this person whom you are bringing with you should be someone who knows you, and you can keep your faith in them. They will be extra support for you. Even when the gaslighter will try to discredit your version of events, that person will be there to take your side. They will reinforce the fact that you are not crazy or you do not imagine things.

If you are facing gaslighting in a social situation, for example, at a party or at a workplace, try not to meet the gaslighter alone. It's always advisable to direct contact as much as possible and even if you do meet him/her, take someone with you.

If the gaslighting is at your workplace and it is your boss who is manipulating you, then you should try your best to limit reporting to him alone. Don't attend any lunches or parties or events that you are not required to. Avoid conversations with the gaslighter in the hallway or the cafeteria when you are alone. A very effective way of disarming the gaslighter (especially when he is your boss) is to build healthy and positive relationships with other superiors or leaders in your company. Build your network with other people who will help you grow and seek out mentors who will recognize your talents and push you forward in the right direction.

Step 4 – Prioritize Self-Esteem

Prioritizing self-esteem is very important because it gives you the strength to stay strong from the inside, and that is a primary requirement if you want to fight the gaslighter. The effects of gaslighting are not only on your own self, but it pretty much creeps into all other parts of your life as well. It can hamper your choice of things or your favorite people. Self-care, in such situations, becomes all the more important because gaslighting can take a huge toll on you both physically and mentally. The more you focus on working on your self-esteem, the more confident you will become.

This, in turn, will make you feel that you can stand up to the gaslighter and deal with anything that comes your way.

Practicing positive affirmations and repeating them every day is even more necessary in people who cannot be happy with themselves and always need some sort of external validation. The moment you give in to external validation, you give the gaslighter one more opportunity to pounce on you. I am not saying that you should not be with any loved one or lean on them for support – it is completely okay and necessary to have a shoulder to cry on. And, at the same time, it is equally important that you value yourself from within and know that 'you are enough.' You do not need anyone to complete you or validate you.

So, the next time you feel that you need someone else to validate your feelings or even a thought, sit down, take a moment, and try to do it yourself. Affirm the perception, thought, or anything else that you were trying to seek external validation for. In the beginning, you might feel intimidating. But don't leave hope. Keep trying, and the more you practice, the easier it will become. With time, you will gain more trust in yourself.

The abuse that you have endured from the gaslighter cannot be described in words, and thus, it is imperative that you engage in self-care. It will not happen overnight because it takes time and patience, and thus, it is a step-by-step process. The most important factor here is time. If you think you are not doing your best or that you are not feeling okay, take a break and don't be too hard o yourself. There will be lots of ups and downs, but you cannot afford to lose yourself in the process. You can also try and spend some me-time. During these hours with yourself, you can do some gardening at home, read a book, listen to your favorite songs, or anything else that gives you happiness and joy. In fact, doing household chores is also something you can do if it brings you happiness. And then there is shopping too! And if nothing seems to work, you can always go for a day out. Whatever you do, make sure you choose activities that are relevant to you and not suggested by some random person on the internet.

Emotional trauma will take time to heal. So, never blame yourself just because it is taking more time. Give yourself a break – you have been through a lot for a consistent period of time. Also, just because you were at the receiving end of the gaslighting doesn't mean that you have something to be ashamed of. Moreover, you need to be aware of what triggers your trauma and be kind to yourself. Sometimes you will be preoccupied with memories of the past, and you will keep ruminating on what had happened – these things are completely normal, so don't be too harsh on yourself. But whenever you catch yourself going back to the painful memories, take a pen and paper and write down all those things that were unfair to you, all those times you were forced to do things you didn't want to do, or every time you were humiliated. This will remind you of all the reasons why you are trying to break this cycle. Reboot yourself as many times as you want because, in the end, it will only make you stronger. Self-care will help you see yourself as the amazing person you are and understand your worth.

Step 5 – Set Healthy Boundaries

Out of all the steps that you have learned in the disarming process, this is one of the most important ones. The whole idea of gaslighting is when a person violates your boundaries, so having healthy boundaries is a must when you want to disarm a gaslighter. You need to decide for yourself how much manipulative behavior you are going to tolerate and when you are going to stand up for yourself. And only thinking about it is not going to work – you need to make a conscious effort. Healthy boundaries will not let you suffer at the hands of the manipulator, and you will be able to protect your sanity and mental peace. Sometimes, the gaslighter is someone very close to you or your family; in that case, severing the relationship completely is not always possible. Even then, you can set healthy boundaries. When there is a proper boundary in place, gaslighters won't be able to influence you like they used to before.

Even if the gaslighter is becoming agitated, try not to give in and stay away from the fight. You should restrict yourself from being available to them. You should always have clarity while communicating your stand in the relationship and who you are as a person. Always remember that there is no use trying to change a gaslighter because they will remain the same, and so, you should refrain from calling them out or explaining how toxic they are. Understand that you should not only maintain a physical distance but psychological distance as well. You do not need anyone to complete you, and so you need to stop giving the gaslighter the power to have control over you. The moment you stop letting your boundaries be compromised, you will be able to break this toxic loop.

When this sort of gaslighting is taking place in your workplace, you need to understand that you have to maintain your distance from the gaslighter, even if it is your boss. You have to imagine yourself to be wearing a protective suit that repels everything negative that comes its way, including the manipulative words of your boss – that's what it means to have healthy boundaries. You need to view them as a separate entity and even if they throw harsh words at you, remind yourself that it is not about you – this will make you feel that they are pathetic! Also, ensure that you take part in as many affirming activities as you can. No matter how tough things get, you need to keep telling yourself that it is your boss who is the psychopath, and you are completely fine. Do things that you love, and this will help you remember who you are at your very core.

Step 6 – Seek Help From Friends and Family

When you are surrounded by people who are trying to gaslight you, there is already a lot of negative energy that you need to deal with. Your overall life starts to seem too toxic. But it will become easier if you have your family or friends to support you. In short, a strong support system can make the recovery process smooth and easy. But it is not only a privilege but also a gift to have such people in your life who will love you for who you are, encourage you to achieve new heights, and simply be there for you through thick and thin. These people are priceless, and you should never lose them. They will never judge you for anything and keep loving you unconditionally. Irrespective of whether you are being gaslighted or not, there will come times in your life when you will feel that it would have been better if you had someone to share your thoughts with, and that is when you need your support system.

You get this warm feeling of belongingness when there is someone to support you through your highs and lows. You feel secure and safe no matter how much you have to struggle in life. You feel valued, loved, heard, and wanted, and all of these feelings are very, very important in life to have a healthy mental state. These feelings will prevent you from being too hard on yourself and will be a constant reminder that you are not alone and that you are loved. It is even therapeutic when there are people in your life who are genuinely thinking about your well-being, and they are always there to help you out. Thus, when it comes to your mental health, your support system plays a vital role in it.

So, these were some of the steps that you can take to disarm the gaslighter and take back control of your own life.

Chapter 5: Recovery Phase 1 – Practicing Acknowledgment and Self-Compassion

Gaslighting is a form of emotional abuse, and when continued for a long period of time, it can cause some seriously detrimental effects to your mental well-being. Everyone wants to be surrounded by people who make them feel wanted, respected and loved, but that is not always the case. We also have manipulators in our society who are waiting for us to lower our boundaries so that they can attack. You have to be very careful of these people. Sometimes, we fail to recognize them because they are people we love, and we never expect them to harm us in any way. So, if you indeed are a victim of gaslighting, recovery is possible, and the first step is to acknowledge the fact that you have been emotionally abused by the gaslighter, and only then can you walk on the path of self-compassion.

In the beginning, you won't even realize that your relationship with the gaslighter is a toxic one or that he/she is trying to manipulate you – everything will seem like the perfect fairy tale until it's not. But keep in mind that gaslighters are extremely good at manipulating, and so they know which qualities to show you at first so that you become emotionally attached to them. With each day you spend in their vicinity, you might feel that you are building a stronger bond, whereas, in reality, the gaslighter is just working towards a larger plan. The abuse will be in full effect by the time you finally notice that the bond you share is not a healthy one. But there is also another scenario to this – there are people who do recognize that they are being manipulated or that something is not right, but they just simply don't want to acknowledge it by giving excuses like 'they were not always like this,' or 'they will change with time,' or 'they are going through a tough time' and so on. So, in this chapter, let me first show you can acknowledge your abuse.

Acknowledge the Abuse

Most of the time, the victim is not aware that he/she is emotionally abused by the gaslighter. So, here are some things that you should be careful of –

- **Your partner always tries to control you by using gaslighting.** You already know what gaslighting looks like but if you want to take a quick look, go to Chapter 1. When you are in an abusive relationship with your partner, they will always try to have the last word and have the upper hand on you. For that, they will use various tactics, one of which is gaslighting. They will always try to make you look like the one at fault and that you don't have the right perception of reality. If you are constantly trying to stand up to your partner by saying 'I never said such things' or 'I never did what you just said,' then the possibility is that your partner is trying to frame you and cause self-doubt. When these things continue for a longer period of time, it is very easy for a person to start losing control over reality, and ultimately they begin questioning themselves.

- **You apologize for things you know you did not do –** When someone is gaslighting you, their primary aim is to make you feel that you are the one at fault no matter what the situation is. They will emotionally abuse you into believing that you are always doing the wrong things and making the wrong decisions even when you are right at your place. When things continue for a long time, you will start blaming yourself for everything that happens and apologize every other second. Deep down, you might know that you were not at fault, but on the outside, you feel that you need to say sorry for being inconsiderate.

- **Even when someone else hurts you, you feel sorry for them –** Gaslighters are one of the best manipulators out there. They spend time analyzing you and know exactly what can be used against you to trigger your feelings. They also know the tactics to play the victim in every case. One of their favorite tactics is to bring up all the trauma they supposedly endured in their childhood years so that everyone in front of them feels sorry for them. When this happens, the actual victim, that is, the person whom the gaslighter is manipulating completely overlooks the negative behavior of the gaslighter and focuses only on the hardships that they have had to face throughout their life. The victims forget the fact that they also have to acknowledge that they have been hurt in this process.

- **Your finances are being controlled by the gaslighter** – Yes, this is a very major problem that people in relationships with gaslighters face. You will often not be allowed to handle your own finances. You will not be allowed to make any purchases until and unless your gaslighter permits you to. Moreover, in extreme situations, the gaslighter might even take away your right to access your bank accounts, and all your passwords will be with them so that you cannot open your accounts without seeking their help. All of these things together give the gaslighter total control of your overall financial state. As you know that finance is an important aspect of living an independent life and if you are deprived of it, the gaslighter indirectly takes away your independence.

- **You always have to inform your whereabouts to the gaslighter** – In the beginning, you might think that the person is simply concerned about your safety, and that is why they keep asking you about your whereabouts, but with time, you will see how it evolves into a kind of control over you. Always remember that it is nothing but emotional abuse when you have to answer to someone for everywhere you go or who you choose to go out with.

- **They always make hurtful jokes about you** – Simply making fun of you or criticizing you under the disguise of sarcasm or joke is not funny and definitely not healthy. This is just another form of abuse that is happening to you in the hands of the gaslighter. The sooner you realize that, the better for you.

But recovery from such kind of emotional abuse and gaslighting is possible, and the first step towards it is acknowledging the abuse itself. Understand and believe in the fact that you don't deserve to put up with such behavior. You deserve to be happy and be with someone better. But all of these changes are not going to happen all of a sudden. You need to work towards it, and with time, your mindset will start changing, and you will engage in self-love. Another thing that is important to understand here is that you cannot change or fix your partner because gaslighters are not willing to do anything about their emotionally abusive ways. In fact, they like to dwell in it, and there is nothing you can do about that.

When you are being gaslighted for a long time, you start questioning your reality and then rationalizing the fact that maybe you are the one at fault. And people often resort to these things rather than acknowledging the abuse because they are mostly scared and upset to accept the fact that someone they love so closely can abuse them emotionally or hurt them so badly. But you need to understand that regardless of the time that you have spent with that person, abuse is abuse. Acknowledging the abuse will help you be softer to yourself and not blame yourself for random things. You will slowly start giving yourself the permission to feel things and emotions that you had suppressed for a long time.

Practicing Self-Compassion

Self-criticism and blaming oneself for the things you didn't even do are some common things victims of gaslighting face. But don't worry, this is not anything that cannot be fixed. You can overcome this habit of criticizing or being too hard on yourself by practicing self-compassion, and that is what we are going to learn in this section. With time, you will see how self-compassion also paves the way for self-acceptance and a much happier life in general.

Gaslighting can change the way you see yourself or think about yourself, but self-compassion can undo this. You have to be understanding and kind to yourself and understand that no one is ever perfect. But with every mistake that you make in life, you open up more possibilities for growth and learning. The actual meaning of self-compassion is to have a nonjudgemental attitude towards yourself where you will be kind and show patience. Unlike what most people think – self-compassion is not linked or the same as selfishness.

Here are some ways in which you can practice self-compassion and walk on the road to recovery from gaslighting –

Indulge in Forgiveness

In gaslighting victims, there is a tendency to blame themselves for everything, irrespective of whether they did anything wrong or not. You need to stop this immediately. Stop blaming and punishing yourself for things you didn't even do. Moreover, what is even more important is that you need to understand that you are a human being, and just like every other human being, you have your shortcomings too. Everyone has their own flaws, and you need to accept your flaws. People who truly love you and respect you love you for the person you are.

The moment you become aware of all of these things, you start realizing that in order to win everyone's love, you do not necessarily have to be a certain way. Having said that, you should also take note of all the times you based your sense of self-worth on perfection or performance.

No matter how much insults the gaslighter is throwing at you, if you can remind yourself that you are enough and that you deserve better, healing will be on its way. You can put up sticky notes in common places with some small affirmations that will remind you throughout the day that you are worthy.

And if you have already broken your relationship with gaslighter but you are lamenting on how you let him/her manipulate you, then don't. It was not your fault. And you cannot let your past ruin your present. You need to move on, and in order to do that, you need to forgive yourself and let your past go.

Practice 3rd Person Self-Talk

This is a very useful healing strategy for victims of gaslighting. Since you have been emotionally abused over a consistent period of time, in the healing phase, your emotions might be heightened thinking about all the wrong that happens to you. But 3rd person self-talk can calm you down and make you feel better. Use this third-person language whenever you are trying to walk you through an emotionally charged situation. It's quite simple. In every sentence where you would have used the pronoun 'I,' say your name. Change all those similar pronouns like 'me' or 'my' and refer to yourself in the third person by using your name.

The more you engage in self-talk, the more you will feel compassion for yourself. This kind of self-talk also encourages your brain to engage in emotional control so that you can think with logic and reason your way out of situations instead of giving in emotionally. With time, if you inculcate this habit, self-compassion will become more and more natural to you. In no time, it will be an automatic response to such situations in your life. But just like everything else, it would take you a lot of practice – you cannot give up. The more compassionate you become, the more positivity you will feel.

Increase Your Desire for Self Preservation

When you have been in a relationship with an abusive person for a long time, and that person kept gaslighting you for years, it takes a heavy toll on your emotional well-being. You become shaken. But for anyone to thrive and live happily, they first need to feel that they are safe. In gaslighting victims, this feeling of being safe is absent. A gaslighter will ask you to sacrifice everything you hold dear so that they themselves can enjoy all the good things and privileges in a relationship. Now, they won't ask you directly. Instead, they will employ covert tactics to do so. When gaslighters gain this control over you, they feel happy, satisfied and somehow also derive pleasure from it.

But this continued behavior often comes at a great cost – and that cost is the victim giving up his/her sense of self-preservation or the desire to remain safe because the only thing on their mind at that point is to please the gaslighter and keep peace in the relationship. This is how things become exploitative and one-sided. Remember that your desire to be safe and feel safe is already present there inside of you – you simply need to find it once again and reignite it.

Strive to Bring About a Change

It's definitely not easy to change the way in which you view your abusive partner. It will not happen overnight and is definitely going to take a lot of time. The most difficult part is to acknowledge that the person you love or the person with whom you have some of the most beautiful and intimate moments of your life has been abusing you emotionally for months. But at the end of the day, you need to remember that you owe it to yourself to change and strive towards going on a path of healing.

Take a Proactive Approach to Get Rid of Negative Self-Talk

We did encourage you to talk to yourself in the third person, but sometimes, people engage in negative self-talk rather than a positive one, and that is something we definitely don't want you to do. When you have been criticized by the gaslighter over and over again, it becomes ingrained in your mind to self-criticize whenever things don't go as planned. But you need to catch yourself doing that and practice self-compassion. Imagine catching someone else engaging in negative self-talk. What would you have done? You would have told them to be positive and not be so hard on themselves, right? Well, the same applies to you as well. Give yourself the empathy and comfort you would have given someone else. Healing can never come from criticizing yourself.

Be Mindful

Self-compassion and mindfulness are very closely interrelated. When you practice being mindful, you don't engage in self-judgment. Mindfulness always requires you to be in the present moment. Healing from gaslighting might make you go through some heightened states of emotions whenever those bad memories come flashing back. But if you don't want that happening, mindfulness can be of real help.

Finally, I'd like to remind you that just like everyone else, you are fully worthy of love. You will have to face some really bad and difficult emotions along the way to healing, but these things are normal. You need to recognize the fact that you are human and keep moving forward. Accept yourself for the person you are, and don't let someone else's word question your reality.

Chapter 6: Recovery Phase 2 – Work on Your Self-Esteem

Gaslighting, in psychological terms, is that abusive emotional technique that parents, partners, friends, siblings, or your colleagues can use as a tactic against you to make you feel incompetent, inferior to them, emotionally incapable, mentally unsound, and to make you feel that your version of the reality is not correct and that somehow it is dependent on them that will solve your problems. The actual reality might be completely different from what these people are trying to portray, but these people have the tendency to gain power over you psychologically, and in that way, when they have taken control over you, they also start to render you incapable physically. Gaslighting is an extremely powerful and effective means of emotionally abusing someone and rendering them handicap psychologically. There resides an intense level of sadistic pleasure on the part of the torturer, who gets satisfaction out of the emotional suffering of the victim.

Most often than not, the gaslighters are completely aware of all their actions, and they do so intentionally. It could also be the case that this is something they have either seen their elders do or have been a victim of that at some point, and that is the reason acting in this way has almost become a norm for them. So, they can't help themselves but exert themselves in this way.

In general, there are no specific rules or set patterns that gaslighters follow. They might try out different behavioral tactics to demean the victim. But in all these cases, what happens, as a result, is that the victim loses all sense of the self. Being with a gaslighter is like getting all your ideas to face dismissal at the very starting without even once being considered. They will do so by twisting your own words against you and making it seem as if it's all your fault. With a prolonged treatment like this, anyone will be at such a stage from where all their energy will be used up, and all that will be left is dejection towards the self. What happens then is that instead of wanting to face such behavior again, the victim prefers to stay quiet. That is because every time the victim goes to speak her mind, the result is not good. A sense of powerlessness starts creeping up inside the victim, and slowly a person forgets who they essentially are. Their entire existence starts revolving around the gaslighter, and there remains no essence of self-esteem.

How Can One's Self-Esteem be Affected When Gaslighted?

It doesn't matter whether the person who is gaslighting you is doing so intentionally or not, but if you are unfortunately on the receiving end, then your sense of self-esteem is sure to suffer a blow due to that. There can be various reasons as to why that happens. We are listing down a few of those points for you so that it becomes easier for you to notice that in the future, be it in your life or that of someone close.

- The abuser will silence you all the time. It is very common for someone who is gaslighting you to not let you have your say and to perpetually silence your voice. They will try to intellectually sabotage you and will not take any of your views and ideas into consideration. This will make you feel inferior giving rise to a sense of disempowerment. It will slowly become a one-sided dominant relationship with you on the receiving end of all the blame and the one who has to decide on his action based on what the other person wants.

- You tend to lose yourself in such a toxic relationship. The more you remain with such a person, the more they are going to mold your life according to how they want it to. And not before long will a time come when you will realize that you don't know who you are anymore. All your decisions will be taken by that other person, and as none of your opinions are given importance, you will get into the habit of not complaining at all with such a treatment. You will become subdued.

- If you are gaslighted, you will be emotionally confused all the time. A gaslighter can be your biggest enemy and your best friend in the span of a minute, and it is bound to make you feel apprehended all the time. That is because you will have to change your behavior according to how they want you to be. That is emotionally stunting and also very insulting. You won't be able to be your true self as all you will be expected out of you is to cater to your abuser's whims and fancies.

- You will know that something is wrong, but you won't be able to point it out. Gaslighters are very cunning. Never for once will they do anything upfront that will give you a chance to accuse them. They plan their activities in a way that even though you know that something is wrong, you won't be able to point it out easily. Even if you go to say anything, they will twist your own words in a way that will make you feel all the more guilty. They will make it seem that they are doing it for your good when in reality, the situation is completely the opposite.

How to Regain One's Self-Esteem?

The first step to recover from gaslighting is to first and foremost recognize your reality. The victim of gaslighting needs to come out of the phase of denial and accept the reality for what it is. No matter who the gaslighter is in one's life, no matter how close or otherwise important they are, until the person truly accepts the truth, there won't be any improvement in their lives. So, once the person has truly accepted the truth and taken the gaslighter for what they actually are, then starts the process of progression. It won't be a very easy journey as the damage that a gaslighter does is usually very deep. But, that being said, once you are ready to accept how things are, it will only be a matter of time before you can come out of that dark stage by taking one step at a time. We are providing you with some tips that we hope will be helpful in defending you from a gaslighter and also help gain your self-esteem back.

- **Do not take responsibility for what others do** – It is a common habit on the part of the gaslighter to blame the entire thing on you if anything happens to go wrong. The more you tend to give in to these false and unfair allegations out of pressure or fear, the more chances the gaslighter will get to repeat it again and again. What they also do is come up with new tactics to make you feel bad. If you deny what they are accusing you of doing, chance sare that they will not waste time in coming up with something new. So, in order not to give in to the strategies and hold your ground, you need to stop taking responsibility for all that the abuser is telling you.

- **Do not give up on your feelings for them** – The next thing that you need to keep in mind is that a gaslighter will never care about how you feel as long as their agenda is fulfilled. That is the reason; if you keep on catering to their whims and fancies, it will be you who will be at a loss as that person will keep on extracting from you emotionally without ever giving anything in return. That is the reason one of the most important ways to get back your self-esteem is to constantly remind yourself that your emotions and feelings matter, and you shouldn't neglect them for anyone.

- **Try to remember your truth** – It is a very common characteristic of a gaslighter to behave in a way that makes the victim question themselves. They are usually very confident about what they believe and what they want, and that is the reason they make sure to be so confident about themselves that the victim has no way but to doubt themselves. And that is where the problem lies. Prolonged ill-treatment in the hands of a gaslighter will then make sure that the victim not only losses out on confidence but also start doubting their own self. A gaslighter can make the victim forget their own truth, which is why they fall prey to the abuses and become helpless. Their self-esteem hits rock bottom because of the fact that they, at all points, have to deal with a person who looks down on them. That is the reason if a person wants to come out of the effects of a gaslighter and regain their sense of self back, they need to come in contact once again with their own reality and own truth. The truth about who they are and where they belong. That they are not what the gaslighter has made them feel for so long. That is the reason, no matter what they say, keep your firm beliefs on what you think is the truth, and do not let go of your position even if they force you to. Keep on reminding yourself that you are a sensible person who can decide what is right and wrong, and you don't need someone else to decide that for you.

- **Do not accept their decisions** – A gaslighter will make sure that they win all the arguments by using their twisted techniques and will try to mold your decisions according to what they want you to do. This treatment of yours, if allowed for a long time, will most definitely make you lose your self-esteem. So, stop accepting what they say when you know that they won't ever be honest with you and will definitely not want your good. Just because they have a particular opinion about you or something related to you doesn't mean that is the truth. It just means that they have an ulterior purpose by making you feel a certain way. If you think that you can talk with them like sensible people usually do, then you are wrong. That is the reason there is no point in trying to argue with them about something. It is better to keep a tight hold on your feelings about things or yourself and not let them encroach them in your private space so that your sense of self-esteem is not hindered.

- **Prioritize your well-being** – You have got to understand that you are the most important person to you, and you need to make sure that you are not jeopardizing your well-being for anyone. The sooner you understand that, the better it will be for you. Staying in contact with a person who is gaslighting you is problematic and traumatic enough. It will invariably lead to psychological violence. That is the reason prioritizing your well-being, and your safety is of prime importance. If you don't do that, both your physical and psychological safety will be in danger. If you are to protect your self-esteem and keep your psychological well-being in proper condition, then you need to take necessary precautions. The moment you understand what that other person is doing to you, it is better to keep a distance from them. You need to give yourself more time to come in contact with your inner self. Be it by spending time with friends and family or doing things that you like. You cannot let go of the things that make you happy just because someone else tells you to.

- **Keep in mind that you are not alone** – It is very natural to feel alone in such a situation when you have a person who has constantly been gaslighting you for a long time, and your sense of self-esteem is in a shambles. You might feel at a loss because all this person has done till now is make you feel bad about yourself. Gaslighting can isolate you completely. You will start feeling you are not worth anything, and that will make you feel conscious about all your actions. That, in turn, will make you distance yourself away from people completely. But the thing is not that. You are never alone. Remember that it is always advisable to seek help if you need it. It is natural to not always be at your best, but in no way does that mean that you lack in something. Be it a friend or a professional, if you think that asking someone for help and talking to someone about your experience will be helpful, then do not defer it. Take that help as soon as possible.

- **Make sure you have proofs** – Make sure that you have adequate proof of what has been happening with you. It is important because a person who has the habit of gaslighting you will never accept the truth because they base their entire life upon their standards of belief and illusions by which they judge others. They will never accept the truth or respect your privacy. So, if you need to grow back your self-esteem, then it is important that you keep enough proof for you to believe in yourself and say what the truth is and also for making others see the truth if at all they don't believe you, a person who has been gaslighting you will invariably have the habit of doing it to others as well. That is the reason you need to keep the proofs so that you always have those for not only for others to see but also for you to look back upon them and take warning to not let that happen with you again in the future and also tell yourself that you have the potential to come out of something toxic. This will greatly boost your self-esteem.

- **Build boundaries** – This is perhaps one of the most important things that we all need to keep in mind before getting ourselves involved in any kind of relationship, no matter who is on the other end. There has to be a certain boundary that we need to set around us if we are to remain independent and in control of our emotions and feelings. Here is a limit that people should maintain and certain limits that nobody should cross. There is a difference between personal and private, and it is better if we let people know how much we are comfortable. The same goes for others with whom we are acquainted. We, too, need to maintain a boundary while dealing with people. In most cases, a person gets the liberty to abuse us because we let them in too much too soon. That is why, if a basic boundary is maintained, both the parties will get time to properly know the other person and decide how far they want to let each other in.

- **Do not blame yourself** – Please remember the fact that you were maltreated or gaslighted is never your fault. This is a thing that is common with gaslighters. They are adept at making everything good about themselves and everything bad about the other person. The more you question yourself, the more it seems that your abuser is doing nothing wrong. And then you genuinely start believing that it is, after all, your fault. That is how gaslighters manipulate you psychologically. Your abuser will want nothing more than to make you feel bad about yourself and to render you so helpless that your self-esteem is shattered. You have got to realize that some people exist because they derive happiness out of other's misery. It is their fault and not yours. However, that being said, what you are responsible for is if you allow that to happen to you regularly, even after knowing the truth. So, stop blaming yourself and start distancing yourself from the concerned person.

- **Be proud of your progress** – We know exactly how much courage it takes to take that step forward out of such an abusive relationship. Such manipulators have their tricks by which they trap people, rendering them unable to move out. So, if you are someone who has taken that step outside, then know this, that we are proud of you. Whatever small steps you have started taking are the ones that will add up to become bigger steps that will set you free. So, celebrate your courage and keep track of it. Keeping track of your progress will give you more incentive to moving forward. So however big or small your progress is, make sure you own it and use that as an example to work harder towards breaking away from that toxic relationship. The other thing that you need to keep in mind is that once you start moving forward, keep that up. Do not stop. Your abuser will try everything in their power to stop your progress from happening. If you stop trying, then all your previous work will amount to nothing. That is why you need to keep moving forward. A little each day. The more you walk ahead, the surer you will be of succeeding.

We hope that by now, you have got a fair idea about how the recovery phase is going to be. It won't be very easy, but it will most definitely not be impossible if you truly want to move forward. Just because you have been abused doesn't mean you shouldn't try now to succeed. You have to try hard no matter how hard it seems because it is your life, and you deserve to be happy. So, don't feel scared to take that first step. Remember that there are many people out there who genuinely want your good, and all you need to do is just put a little more trust in these people and, most importantly, in yourself for you to succeed.

Chapter 7: Recovery Phase 3 – Build Healthy Boundaries

Until and unless you have been the victim of gaslighting in life, you'll never realize that someone can make you feel so inferior and hollow from within. You will keep second-guessing all your steps, your memories, and your perception of things. And it's quite natural to feel devastated, overwhelming, and wonder whether it is you who is going crazy.

Here's How Gaslighting Violates Your Boundaries

You have probably already come across the fact that gaslighting is a form of manipulation that involves violating your boundaries. But I have come to realize that even though people are aware of this situation, they are not aware as to how these boundaries are violated. So, I've noted down some of the common ways in which gaslighters violate and disrespect your boundaries.

Lying

The first and foremost way in which gaslighters disregard your boundaries is by blatantly lying to you. Most of the gaslighting techniques they use are based on one single aspect – lies. In fact, they act like compulsive liars, but the only difference is that behind every lie, they have an ulterior motive. They might lie to you about very insignificant and meaningless things and very important things as well. A very common example is when they did not do what you asked them to do, say taking the dog for a walk, and they would keep insisting on the fact that they did it. Even if you show them evidence that proves otherwise, they will stick to their point and continue lying confidently.

When someone engages in such behavior, they are crossing your mental boundaries. With time, you will slowly start to question your senses and your perception. You start thinking about whether your methods and how you know what you know is wrong. Everything you see with your eyes, smell with your nose, or hear with your ears will now be brought to question in your own mind. You question your reasoning skills too.

Labeling Hurtful Comments As a Joke

This is a very common way that gaslighters use to cross your boundaries and hurt you. At first, they will make a comment about you that is offending, and when you realize it and call them out on it or even if someone else calls them out, they will simply use phrases like 'you are such a softy' or that they were 'just joking.'

In these moments, when they throw that hurtful comment at you, they are actually telling you what they think and then immediately masking it with a lie. When they tell you things like 'you are looking fat,' they said it to hurt you intentionally. And right in the next moment, when they say 'I was only joking,' that's a lie. They want you to believe that what they said initially was only a joke, whereas, in reality, they meant every word so that you get hurt.

Now, this scenario is definitely crossing a person's boundaries. Think about situations when such things happened – people have this inherent tendency to know when a person is actually complimenting you and when they are teasing you. This happens in your subconscious when your brain collects evidence from very subtle things and body sensations that you might not be consciously thinking about. It might even be difficult to put into words how you know that the gaslighter is lying when they say, 'I was just joking.' This inability to explain or prove that they were indeed not lying gives the gaslighter the upper hand, and they continue labeling every hurtful comment as a joke and keep invading your mental boundaries.

Changing Expectations Suddenly Claiming That They Were the Same Since the Beginning

Every relationship has some expectations in them. But a gaslighter will keep changing these expectations all of a sudden, and they won't even discuss it with you. These types of incidents not only constitute material boundary-crossing but also invading mental boundaries.

Here's an example to make the situation clearer to you – suppose you are sharing the flat with another person and both you and your roommate decide that you will equally share all housecleaning tasks and bills. But your roommate comes and tells you that they are too busy with something else, and so, you should do all the household chores. If you try and call them out on it, they might tell you that 'it has always been like this, and I can't figure out why you are making it such a big issue.' That is why t is always advised that whenever you get a new roommate, get every rule in writing so that no one can ever ignore or change them suddenly.

If you are wondering how such things cross your boundaries, well, you are not only being asked to provide much more than you had agreed to, but you are also deliberately forced to question your own memory.

Accusing You Vaguely That You Have Not Been Able to Keep Up With the Expectations

It is in the nature of gaslighters to make meaningless and vague accusations against their victims without any explanation at all. They will not even define what they are accusing you of, thus leaving you in the dark. These types of situations arise when you give your own needs the first priority, and the gaslighter starts to think that they are losing their hold on you. This thought threatens them, and thus, they resort to vague accusations to put you down.

Let us say that you are married to a gaslighter, and now you have a child with them. You also want to work so you get a part-time job.

The moment the gaslighter feels that you are trying to do something for yourself, they will make comments like, 'I always thought you are going to be a good mother, but now I think I was wrong.' No matter how much you try to make them understand that you are only trying to bring more money into the family for a better quality of life, they won't understand and simply keep accusing you. When you tell them all of these things, the gaslighter might even say that they didn't mean all of that and, in turn, ask you what a good mother means. Even if y you tell them to define it, they will distort the definition in a way to fulfill their ulterior motives.

This is another very common example of how a gaslighter crosses your mental boundaries. You already know what it means to be a good mother, but your gaslighter will nonetheless try to make you question yourself. Their main aim is to make you feel that you are not capable of keeping up with the promises that you had made in the past. Thus, it also means that the gaslighter is trying to cross material boundaries so that you start devoting more attention to them, giving them not only time but also material things like money. This increased amount of things is usually far beyond what you are willing to do for them.

Making You Feel Responsible For Their Actions, Thoughts, and Feelings

We all face disagreements in our day-to-day lives, but a healthy way to sort through them is to engage in a conversation. But when you are in a disagreement with a gaslighter, they will always put the blame on you and make you responsible for their actions, thoughts, and feelings. These situations occur even more when you have identified the gaslighting tactics of the gaslighter and trying to set solid boundaries.

Let us see a scenario where this same system of boundary invasion happens. Suppose the gaslighter in your life is your parent. You wanted to learn French, and so you signed up for a class that takes place on Friday nights. But on Friday nights, you used to go to dinner with your parent. In a healthy relationship, the parent would encourage you to learn French. But if your parent is a gaslighter, then they might tell you things like 'You have abandoned me' or 'You no longer care about me' or such things where you will feel guilty or responsible. Now, even if you tell them to go for dinner on some other date, that will interfere with what they want; thus, it won't matter to them. There is often no logic or reason behind the things the gaslighter wants to achieve. Their only aim is to put their own needs first and to make sure you are always under their control. This is crossing several boundaries at once – material, emotional, and mental.

Expecting You to Portray Them As a Very Good Person in Public

This type of boundary crossing is often witnessed in work situations. When your boss is your gaslighter, no matter how rudely they behave with you, they will always want you to uphold them as a very good and idealized person. It's somehow your part of the job to not speak ill of your boss or your company and silently put up with all the wrong things they do. But this shouldn't be the case, right? Since the gaslighter is expecting you to lie in front of everyone, they are firstly crossing material boundaries. And they are also not telling you about your role in their existence, and this comprises of crossing mental boundaries.

They Will Publicly Shame You

In the previous point, I explained how the gaslighter wants you to always speak good of them. At the same time, they will publicly shame you and put you down in any way possible. They will go to great lengths to achieve it, even if it means humiliating you. They will label you with terms like worthless or incompetent in front of everyone. This is something that makes everyone quiver, and it is very abusive in nature too. This type of boundary crossing is done in cases of domestic violence and also in educational and business setups. This type of behavior hits you deep in your heart and crosses your emotional boundaries. Apart from this, since the gaslighter does this in public, it also violates your privacy.

As you must have noticed in all of the cases above, the ultimate aim of the gaslighter is to gain the upper hand on you. But you can prevent that from happening by setting firm boundaries, and I am going to show you how you can do that in the next section. So, read on to find out.

How to Set Boundaries to Protect Yourself?

Setting boundaries is crucial not only to protect yourself from the gaslighter but also to maintain good mental health and establish your identity. Here are some tips that will help you in the process.

Name Your Feelings and Limits

Before you set your healthy boundaries, you need to understand where your limit lies. At the same time, you also have to name your feelings and emotions that you get after a situation. Once you identify your feelings, it will help you understand who you need to set your boundaries with and what situations can affect those boundaries. So, start by identifying what is making you feel stressed or uncomfortable and how much of that situation you can tolerate. Your own emotions in different situations will act as your guideposts while setting these boundaries, and in very simple words, you will gain literacy about your feelings instead of shoving them in a corner or ignoring them.

Be Assertive

The next most crucial step of creating boundaries is to state them boldly and assertively. With some people, you don't always need to be too assertive or use a clear-cut dialogue to maintain your boundaries because they understand why you are doing what you are doing. This mostly happens with people with whom you share a general approach towards life.

On the other hand, when dealing with a gaslighter, they will always try to violate your boundaries, and their main aim is not to allow you to have healthy boundaries. Thinking that you want to set firm boundaries is obviously step 1, but in order to implement it, you also have to be vocal about it with the gaslighter.

However, for people who are not usually vocal or assertive about their own needs, being assertive about their boundaries all of a sudden can be a very intimidating and scary thing to do. So, you need to take baby steps, and ultimately, you will be able to accomplish building healthy boundaries in no time. Start with situations that are more manageable and then work your way up to the challenging ones.

If a work colleague is your gaslighter and the trying to burden you with work and, at the same time, not giving you credit for it, then you can simply tell him/her that you cannot do that work because it is totally out of your expertise. Or, you can also tell them that you have a lot of your own work to do and that you wouldn't be able to make time for them

Permit Yourself to Set Boundaries

Some of us don't face any problems while setting boundaries, but others might feel like they are being selfish and only thinking about their own gains. And then, some people also are afraid of how the other person is going to react once they say that they want to set boundaries.

A very important part of having healthy boundaries in place is learning to say no, but most of the time, people are guilty of saying no to their close ones because they always feel like they are not their best selves when they deny people something.

So, you need to remind yourself that you are not selfish by wishing to set boundaries. Boundaries are a form of self-respect, and they help to maintain a healthy relationship between two people. Thus, if you want to be able to set boundaries, you need to give yourself permission to do so.

Remember that Boundaries Can be Flexible

One thing that people often fail to understand that boundaries are not always the same for everyone. If your boundaries for one person are very stringent, it might not have the same level of strictness for another person. So, the idea is to have different types of boundaries for different people in your life. These boundaries might even change with time, depending on how the person is behaving with you. The boundaries also change as your relationship with the person evolves. So, the right way to set effective and healthy boundaries is to check in with yourself from time to time to understand how you feel about a person and then adjusting your boundaries accordingly.

Lastly, remember that the process of setting boundaries will be effective only when you understand that it is, in fact, a two-way road. Just because the gaslighter is violating your boundaries or manipulating you doesn't mean that you are going to deal with the situation by lashing out or mirroring their behavior. If you violate the boundaries of the gaslighter, in turn, it would only lead to more and more conflict, and the situation will keep escalating without any solution. When the violation of boundaries becomes deep-rooted in your subconscious, it might take you some time to set healthy boundaries, but with practice, it is not impossible.

Chapter 8: A Step-by-Step Approach to Heal From Emotional and Psychological Abuse

Gaslighting is a form of psychological and emotional abuse, and even though you might not find any physical bruises on your body, it scars your mind and leaves behind wounds in your heart that linger for a long time. Moreover, both your physical well-being and behavior and interaction with others are affected when you are exposed to emotional abuse like gaslighting over a long period of time. But it doesn't have to leave a permanent imprint on you because there are some steps that you can follow to walk on the path of healing, and we are going to discuss those steps in this chapter.

Step 1 – Acknowledge What Happened to You

The first step to healing is acknowledging the emotional trauma – without that, you cannot walk towards a better life. Thinking about all those bad memories is not an easy task, but if you want to heal, that's the first thing that you have to do.

But remember that if you are finding it difficult, it's perfectly normal and that you are not alone in this. There are several people who find it difficult, just like you. This is mostly because the idea of feeling shameful because you were emotionally abused is so ingrained in our society that many people try to cover it up and say they are fine when they are not. And another common reason for not acknowledging such things is that people think if they let it be and not think about it, it will go away on its own – but it doesn't happen that way.

One thing that I can tell you for sure is that the more you keep shoving your abuse to the side and ignore it, the more will be your emotional pain, and it will take you an even longer time to heal. Your life will slowly start to crumble down because of the negative effects of this abuse. But the moment you take the first step towards acknowledging it, you will feel a power rise within you – as if you are liberated from something.

Remember that if you feel those same painful emotions as you felt during the abuse during the process of acknowledgment, it is completely normal. These emotions were buried deep inside you, and now it's time for them to come out. Until and unless you allow these emotions to move through you, you won't be able to feel them.

Step 2 – Change Your Negative Thinking Patterns

When you have a gaslighter in your life, that person will always keep trying to change your version of reality or make you question what you think is true. They will keep doing this until and unless you start believing whatever they say without asking any questions. In short, you give more importance to their version of reality than your own. When this goes on for a long time, you slowly start to crumble, and it affects how you see yourself or how you hold yourself in society. Your self-talk takes a negative turn. So, the second most important step of healing is challenging your negative self-talk and correcting all the negative thinking patterns that you have adapted after the abuse.

Some of the common negative thinking patterns that victims of gaslighting adopt are –

- **Black and white thinking** – The gaslighter distorts your reality so much and humiliates you whenever they get a chance that you give in to black and white thinking. In simple terms, you start believing that you can be either a complete failure at things or you get it right. In most cases, you go with the former because that's what your gaslighter thinks.

- **Not considering the positive side of things** – Gaslighters manipulate their victims so much that after a certain point of time, those victims start thinking that nothing good is ever going to happen with them and that

they are never doing anything right. They simply start not
seeing the good side of things and only focus on the negative.

- **Over-generalization** – Since the victims have faced a lot
of bad behavior and abuse at the hands of the gaslighter, they
start over-generalizing everyone they meet. Let us say that
the gaslighter in their life was their romantic partner. Then,
while pursuing future relationships, they might be of the
mentality that all men are the same just because they were in
a relationship with a gaslighter in the past.

- **Name-calling** – In general, name-calling is a tactic that
gaslighters use on victims, and with time, they make the
victim believe those names. After a certain stage, the victim
will start calling those names to themselves as well. For
example, if the gaslighter used to tell them that they are
stupid and make childish decisions, then the victim will start
believing those things when they are exposed to those harsh
comments every day. And there will be a point where they
will start calling themselves stupid even when they made the
right decisions.

- **Self-blame** – The gaslighter's main aim is to keep you
under his/her control at all times, so whenever something
happens, they will try to put the blame on you even if you
had nothing to do with the incident. Similar to name-calling,
when this blame game continues for a long time, the victim
will start engaging in self-blame tendencies and say things
like 'it's all my fault' at all times.

- **False permanence** – When you are in a relationship with
a gaslighter, and you tried to change that person for the
better for a long time but didn't see any results, it's very
natural for you to lose hope. But when you reach that point,
negative thoughts like false permanence start creeping. Thus,
you start thinking that things are going to remain this bad
forever and that you are never going to be with someone who
will treat you well.

All of these negative patterns lead to feelings of guilt, shame, depression, and anxiety. If you let these negative patterns take root in your life, they will destroy everything. So, you should identify these patterns and then start replacing them with healthy and good thought processes.

Step 3 – Practice Self-Care

Step 3 very important to your process of healing. When you have been a victim of gaslighting, it is no secret how much emotional trauma you had to go through, and its impact is still bothering you in life. So, taking care of yourself should be your first priority. When you engage in self-care, you feel like you have a lot more support and energy in your life.

For starters, embrace all the things that you want to do for yourself. Previously, you were more engrossed in doing things that kept your abuser happy, and now, you need to revisit your own hobbies and passions. It can be anything, but doing something for yourself will make you satisfied and happy. There are so many options that you can pursue, and this often leaves people procrastinating. So, the best thing you can do is start small. The more you do these things, the more you will be able to connect with your authentic self.

Self-care also means eating right and giving your body the nutrients it needs. Emotional abuse can lead you to skip your meals. And, when you don't eat right, you have much less energy in you, and your metabolism suffers.

Aside from taking care of your nutrition, the next thing that you should do is engage in some physical exercise. It can be yoga, a simple running session, or even hitting the gym. Make a routine and follow it every day. This will give you a sense of control over your life. When you have been a victim of gaslighting, the abuser had total control of everything in your life. But getting back to a routine means reclaiming that control. Practice waking up at the same time and going to bed at the same time every day. Apart from this, have a relaxing evening routine to distress from the day's activities and calm your mind and body.

Step 4 – Allow Others to Support You

It's good that you are healing from all the trauma in your life, but your journey doesn't necessarily have to be alone. Being gaslighted by someone close to you can leave you scarred, and you end up not putting your faith in anyone ever again. But keep in mind that there are always people in your life who love you and want only the best for you. It can be your friends or even family members. They will be there for you as you work through your own problems. Their presence alone can be very comforting for you, even though you might not recognize it at first.

The first thing about healing is that you don't have to do anything that you feel like not doing. But when you have close friends and family by your side, they can listen to what you feel and not pass any nasty comments and judgmental looks. This empathy is what you need during the process of healing.

If you think you do not have such people in your life, then a better option would be to join a support group where you will find several other people like you who are recovering from gaslighting or other forms of emotional abuse.

It is natural for gaslighting victims to feel isolated from others because that's what a gaslighter does to you. But the more you mix socially with others, you will realize that you are not alone. When you have a safe network of people around you to help you or listen to you when you cry or answer your questions, healing becomes a lot easier.

These are the four main steps towards healing. But in the end, you should not forget that healing takes time so remind yourself that there's no rush. Take all the time you need. When you understand that it will take a significant time to process all those stuffed-up emotions and trauma, healing, as a process, becomes more enjoyable. It is very common and rather easy for people to be harsh on themselves and beat themselves up just because they are not getting results fast. They have been subjected to self-blame for so long that they are very quick to come to the conclusion that healing is not their cup of tea. The only way out of this is to keep reminding yourself that healing is indeed possible, and it takes time. Talking with people who have been through what you are going through helps victims battle this feeling, and they don't berate themselves as much.

Chapter 9: Writing Exercises That Will Help in Healing

Before we go into the topic in detail, let us first create a context, so we know where all this is coming from and why we need a solution for it. We shall then go into how writing can be of great help in such situations. By now, you should have a pretty good idea of what gaslighting is and that it is a kind of mental or emotional experience of abuse faced by a person when someone else experiences manipulates them and distracts them from what is important to them and uses these base tricks to change and maimed the truth so that the concerned person starts questioning what their reality looks like. It leads to serious psychological discomfort and can give rise to many serious problems physical and psychological. This can happen between family members or in between colleagues in the office, or even between friends. That is the reason a substantial amount of precaution needs to be taken so as to keep oneself prepared if such a condition occurs. If anyone is the victim of such a treatment, they tend to lose their sense of confidence, and the relationship is sure to become an abusive one.

Gaslighting is very harmful, and it can truly have horrific consequences. The person who is the victim of such a treatment will start questioning all their actions, and an inherent inferiority complex is what will take away their spirit. As far as short-term consequences are concerned, they will make a person feel helpless and at a loss as to how to conduct oneself in that situation. In most cases, a person might not even understand what's happening before it is too late, and in the long-term, a person is sure to face serious self-esteem issues, which will make regular functioning for them very difficult as all their actions will be affected by that making them incompetent both at a personal and professional level. With a prolonged experience of being a victim of gaslighting, a person could lose his sense of the self so much that they might start believing in other's opinion of abilities more than that of there's, thus becoming dependent on others emotionally. They might also become victims of other psychological problems like clinical depression or Post Traumatic Stress Disorder, or they might have to face memory problems and anxiety disorders. This will make them lack hugely in relationships of every kind, making them almost emotionally tainted.

Can Writing Help to Heal?

Writing is a multi-purpose thing that usually comes in handy to various people for a host of reasons, and there is no end to much help writing can actually be. In the most obvious case, we usually use writing for communication and getting people's attention on something which might be otherwise not possible to convey verbally. For many people who have difficulty expressing themselves vocally, writing has forever been a medium of being honest with themselves and relating themselves with others. Writing is also something that is no stranger to psychological therapy. It is one of the choicest methods of psychotherapists to encourage their patients to try and express themselves through writing because that tends to be immensely helpful in taking out the hidden angst in people, and it works as a healing process altogether. That is the reason, to deal with a situation of gaslighting, writing can actually be a very prominent helpful procedure.

With new medical theories coming up and technology truly advancing, it has been medically proven that writing surpasses its benefits when it comes to healing the mind and can successfully do so even in the case of physical benefits to people who are suffering from even life-threatening conditions. If any patient is suffering from serious cases like AIDS or HIV or asthma, or even arthritis, writing about emotions and stress that the patient might be going through can be of great help to boost one's immune functioning of the body. The main argument behind using writing as a healing method is how effectively a person can use it to their benefit. And for that, the primary step is to understand oneself and one's emotions very well. Only then can a person truly bring what's inside them out on paper and do justice to their emotions. The enlightenment that an honest piece of writing can bring is equal to the verbal solutions given in psychotherapies. So, if a person is consistent in writing, then not only will it help that person to get better it will also help that person from not getting his condition worse.

What happens in an abusive relationship is that there accumulates a lot of pent-up anxieties and pain, which, if not let out, makes the situation worse for the sufferer. What writing does is give a shape to these emotions and help the person understand their way around those emotions, helping them find solutions to the issues they are facing and help reduce the anxiety and pain. Talking about a specific thing repeatedly won't really bring any solution if active steps for growth are not taken. And that is the reason many times when w don't find meaning in our actions, we are able to find meaning in our words, and that is where language comes in help. It helps us realize ourselves better and comes to our rescue. People who are not comfortable being vulnerable while talking tend to not express how they feel due to a lack of communication. But if those same people express themselves through writing, life will become easier for them and the people around them. Writing helps a person get in touch with the healing power that is in all of us as from pen and paper, it helps clarity reach our mind, and that helps create a bond between our intellectual and emotional self. That entire process is very therapeutic.

It is then very important to know how to be expressive while writing so that it helps us heal. We suggest five very simple steps by which expressive writing can be possible. At first comes "*What?*" ask yourself what that thing is that is bothering you at the moment is. Name it. The next thing that we need you to do is to "*Reflect*" or "*Review.*" Calm yourself, whatever you are feeling at that moment, be true to those emotions and then reflect upon the thing that you want to write about. The next step is to "*Investigate.*" Sit with your emotions. It won't be easy at the beginning, but you will get there. Investigate all the feelings that you have regarding the concerned matter. "*Time*" comes next. You need to fix yourself a particular time for you to sit every day and diligently write about it. Write whatever you feel and what comes to your mind. So not hide anything that you might be feeling at that moment. Try to maintain this time regularly and not break your habit. Lastly, *"End"* this exercise by re-reading your written thoughts and summarizing your feeling at the end.

Some Writing Prompts That Can Be Helpful

It is true that writing is a major therapeutic way in dealing with recovering from an abusive or a toxic relationship. Once we take the decision of making our lives better, the next question that comes up is how to do that. That is why we are providing you with some prompts that we hope will be helpful.

1. Let's start with day one. It is important that we take one day at a time when we want our problem to be cleansed from deep within. On the first day, let us start by asking ourselves what the things that we need to address are and why do we think they are causing agony in us in the first place. Let us then start from the beginning, which is our childhood. Let us write about what kind of a childhood we had and what are our first thoughts regarding the experiences we had then. It is important that we honestly write what is causing us emotional stress.

2. That brings us to day two. What we advise you to do on this day is to come back to the present and write about your biggest emotional needs now and from whom do you expect them. Write whether these needs are unfulfilled and whether there is a lack of reciprocation of something in your life from someone. Now, I will need you to go back to your childhood memories once again and analyze for yourself whether there was a time in your childhood when you had felt the lack of reciprocation from people of these same emotions that you are feeling now and what needs that gave rise in you.

3. Day three will need you to be a bit more creative. We need you to picture your emotions on paper. Draw the feelings inside you and give them their due recognition. Use appropriate metaphors and descriptive pictures to convey

your feelings. The moment you start noticing your feelings, they will start making more sense.

4. On day four, we want you to come face to face with your pent-up anger. The more you neglect your anger and let it accumulate, the more it will harm you and make you ill. So take this day to write about all the anger you have. Identify who those people are who make you angry and take your time in formulating a letter addressed to these people. Remember that this letter is not to be sent, but it is just a means for you to let it all out.

5. Take the entire day five to continue with these letters. Do not hurry, and most importantly, do not leave anything out. Be honest with yourself and finish these letters.

6. On day six, we want you to make a list of such needs in you which are unmet and unfulfilled, which you think you can't fulfill yourself. Ask yourself what limitations you think you have and make a list of all those things which you think prevent you from making your decisions and living life the way you want to.

7. On the seventh day, go back to your childhood and reflect back on all the people you had around you then and find out if there is any memory of anyone of them crossing their boundaries with you and being abusive. Write about them and those memories. Also, write about members who were absent and whose presence bothered you the most. We then want you to make a comparison of your current family situation and make a note of the same above-mentioned things.

8. Take days eight and nine to make a list of all the things you think you have done wrong with yourself and let wrong things happen with you. And also, try and remember all the good things and make a list of them when you have felt happy about yourself and the positive steps that you have

taken in your life. Write an honest letter to your younger self who went through pain. See what advice you would give to yourself.

9. Make a list of all those people whom you think you have wronged in your life and write about why you think so. Take some time and write candid letters to all those whom you think you could have treated better.

10. The final step then is to try and move forward as you get an overall idea of every aspect of yourself.

What is important to understand is that you will only benefit from writing if you are honest with yourself and if you want to move forward. As long as you remain fixed with the negativities, it won't be possible for you to accept your reality. As you accept your reality, both your past and your future will get in line for you to deal with them maturely and live a better life. I hope that this has been helpful.

Chapter 10: Protecting Yourself Against Manipulators in Everyday Life

In today's world, there are manipulators everywhere around you. Most of the people around you are looking for evil ways to take advantage of you for their own twisted pleasures. You need to be very conscious all the time if you want to protect yourself from manipulators. In this article, I am going to talk about several ways by following which you will be able to protect yourself from all the manipulators out there in your everyday life.

Stop Falling Into Their Traps

Interrogating you, blaming you, and confusing you are their tactics of getting under your skin; they will do all sorts of things just to make you fall into their trap. Make sure not to fall for their words. They will pretend to be nice in front of you and try to make you feel bad or guilty about something you have nothing to do with. You might even end up apologizing to them for something you didn't even do. Don't let it happen. In case you have to deal with manipulators every day (in your institutions or workplace), make sure to ignore them as much as you can. If you can't ignore them, simply surprise them with a positive attitude and don't keep a combative attitude. In this way, they will get confused too as to why their tricks aren't working for you, and they might even stop experimenting with their evil tricks on you in the future.

Start Noting Down Everything They Say While Conversing With You

Emotional manipulators have a habit of twisting and turning words just to make you seem like the bad guy. After doing or saying something bad, they might act, do, or say things in such a way that you might feel that you misunderstood them and feel guilty for doing so. Even if it seems like a little too much, still make sure to note down every detail of whatever that person says to you. In this way, you can identify whenever the manipulator changes any detail according to their convenience just to make you look bad. Sometimes, they may completely deny the fact that they said or did a particular thing in order to make you feel bad or guilty. If you have everything written, you will be able to get clarity on what is right and what is wrong and can save yourself from a lot of hassles. This is a smart technique of saving yourself from unwanted drama.

Try Steering Clear Whenever It is Possible

Imagine having no manipulator in your circle! How amazing would that be! Whenever you meet a person for the first time, try to look at the red flags very carefully. If you see anything negative about their vibe or energy, make sure to fully avoid your interactions with them in the future. In this way, you will have absolutely no manipulator in your life, and you will be spared from a lot of unnecessary hassles. In some cases, totally avoiding the manipulator is tough. This is when the manipulator is from somewhere that you can't ignore fully, like the workplace, schools, colleges, or even family. In these cases, try to limit your interactions with them as much as possible. Also, make sure that your interactions are strictly based on formal things. For example, if that person asks you something related to work. Either try to ignore it or keep your conversations limited to work-related things only. Don't get too friendly or too close. This can give him a lot of chances to emotionally exploit you. Don't start talking informally; otherwise, it will cost you later.

Try Keeping a Backup

Manipulative people often get scared of playing their dirty tricks when a lot of people are around them. They mainly do these things when you are kind of alone with them and when their activities are not seen by anyone else. So, if it is impossible for you to completely shut them out of your life, or cut down on your interactions with them, try to be around as many people you can while dealing with them. When others are around you, the manipulators will think twice before saying or doing something weird. They will be too conscious about what others will think of them. Therefore, you won't have to deal with it. It is a good way to save yourself from them if you find it hard to fight alone.

Start Calling Them Out on Their Behavior

All manipulators are basically coward; that is why they get pleasure by hurting others. They love playing mind games and love to see whenever people fall into their traps. One thing that every manipulator hate is confrontation. They don't like being called out or being confronted about their behaviors. So, whenever you see that someone is trying to manipulate you emotionally, directly call them out on their behavior. This will allow you to catch them off-guard. Take your own stand and say to them directly that their words or actions are making you feel uncomfortable and that you don't want to deal with these anymore. They might try to deny that they said or did those things, but you could still have satisfaction knowing that you stood up for yourself and didn't just endure everything like a weak person. This satisfaction will give you more courage to confront again in the future. If you keep confronting them and calling out their names, they might stop doing their evil tricks on you because they will understand that you aren't a weak person who will just go on tolerating everything and get played every time.

Don't Get Emotionally Attached to Them

Emotional manipulators take advantage of those who get emotionally attached to them. They use this as their weapon to do anything they want with you as they know you wouldn't be able to say no to them. I have seen a lot of cases where people keep enduring everything just because they are emotionally attached to that person. Make sure not to do this. This is because when you get too emotionally attached, either you don't see the bad side in them and ignore all the red flags, or you keep forgiving them and expecting them to change even when you know that isn't going to happen.

A lot of times, the emotional manipulator is someone close to you, like your partner or a friend. This makes it hard for you to ignore them or confront them or even think of leaving them because they matter to you. For avoiding these kinds of situations, try staying conscious from the beginning so that you don't get too emotionally attached to someone who might manipulate you emotionally in the future. When you see that they are steamrolling your emotions completely, see this as a red flag. Back away slowly from the relationship and let them know about your boundaries. In case if it is someone from your workplace or someone from the family, make sure to keep a civil and cordial relationship with them.

Try Meditating Often

Relaxation techniques like meditation often help you to release stress and gain inner peace. When you have inner peace, you see things clearly with a calm mind. No matter how much chaotic your surrounding situations are, you will be able to deal with the manipulators and their tricks calmly. When you meditate and gain inner peace, you might also start seeing their struggles and reasons behind their behaviors. This might also lead you to see them with the eyes of compassion and pity. This will help you to forgive them and see the good in them. You might see the bigger picture and deal with them in a kind way. This will save you from a lot of trouble. Sometimes kindness is all you need to rise above someone. You instantly become the bigger person when you forgive someone and look at them with pity. Also, make sure that you only forgive them and not forget what they did. Forgetting what they did will put you in the same place again, so don't do that. Forgive and move on with your life.

Try Inspiring Them

Inspiring someone is the best thing that you can do. Manipulators are humans, too, and there might be some reasons behind these kinds of behavior. Try to see the good in them and inspire them. You might inspire them not to waste their time messing around with people and invest their time in bettering themselves, eating healthy, staying fit, chasing their dreams, and doing everything in order to be the best versions of themselves. If they truly get inspired by you, they won't be the same person again. After all, everybody makes mistakes, and everyone deserves a second chance. You should give it to them and see if they change. The most important thing that you need to keep in mind here that it is not your duty to inspire them or change them. If you see that no matter what you do, they are not changing, or it is taking a toll on your mental health to inspire them or make them a better person, you don't need to do it. Nothing is more important than your well-being.

Try Not to Get Too Empathetic

Empathy is good, but too much of it can bring you trouble. As I have mentioned earlier, that you need to be a better person and try to inspire them; you also need to keep in mind that it is not your duty to do so. If you see that the person isn't putting any effort into bringing the change, don't waste your time. Some people just never change, and it might be a little hard to accept, but it is a fact, and you should accept it. Just move on already!

Start Telling Them That They Are Right

Telling someone that they are right even when you know they don't need a lot of courage. Your ego will crash to do so, but if you can do it, you will satisfy your soul. Emotional manipulators crave drama. They want you to get back at them with a combative attitude so that they can again twist your words and play them against you to make you feel worse. Once you say "yes, you are right," they will have nothing more to say. This will catch them off-guard, and they will be confused for a while about what to say or do next in order to continue this. Sometimes saying someone they are right makes you a bigger person, and this pisses off the other party. Letting them win the argument will not only maintain your inner peace but will also show them that you aren't someone who will waste your energy, effort, or time just to win a stupid little argument with them. Surprise them with this positive attitude, and they will understand that you aren't easy to mess with, and they will make sure to keep their distance from you in the future.

Try Letting Go of the Harmful Relationships

If you start noticing these kinds of behaviors in your spouse, girlfriend, or boyfriend, leave them then and there. Don't stay for the sake of love because love has no room for manipulation. Nobody is worth more than your own happiness and well-being. A person can't be changed forcefully if they are not willing to. Try talking to them about it once and see if they are making efforts to change. If yes, very well, but if not, just leave right away! You deserve someone who will love you, care for you, cherish you, and help you be a better person, not someone who will take advantage of you or will make you feel miserable about yourself. If your partner does this, then you must know that he/she is not in love with you. They are just with you because you seem to be easy prey to them. So, make sure not to be in any kind of relationship with a manipulator. If you start explaining to them why you are leaving, they might turn that against you as well. This will again damage your mental peace and make things worse for you. Always remember that you don't need to explain anything to a person who doesn't care about you. Leave silently, and they will know exactly why you did what you did.

Develop a Strong Mentality

Never let a manipulator get inside your skin, don't let their words into your heart, and don't let their dirty tricks get inside your head. Remembering these three things can be a life-changer for you. Manipulators get inside your head for making you do or feel what they want you to do or feel. If they can't get inside your head, they might as well stop bothering you. Know that you are valuable and that your emotions and feelings are not something to play with. While dealing with a manipulator, keep your head straight and don't let their tricks get the better of you. Ignore whatever they are saying or trying to do. Know your self-worth and keep your mind strong. Once you are able to do that, nothing can bring you down.

Practice Positive Self-Talk

Sometimes all you need is a little affirmation from yourself. People are often too harsh on themselves and forget to remind themselves about how good they actually are. Always remember that you deserve the same amount of kindness that you give to others. Don't blame yourself for everything, and don't just keep feeling guilty for every single thing. You are worth a lot more, and you should know it. Practicing positive self-talk is a great way of boosting your self-worth. Make sure to say positive things about yourself in your mind every single day. You will understand how good of a person you are. Once you know your self-worth, you won't be bothered by these cheap tricks of the manipulators around you. Give yourself positive and uplifting affirmations every day like "I am amazing," "I deserve all the good things," "I am much more than what they think of me," "What they say about me isn't going to bother me because I know who I am." These affirmations will make sure to make you realize your own value and give you the courage to throw those people away who don't give you the respect and love you deserve.

Manipulators are everywhere around you. You need to keep your eyes open to see the red flags. Don't make the mistake of ignoring the signs. Don't get intimidated by them and give in to their manipulation. Work on your self-confidence, be strong, and know your self-worth. This will give you the courage to stand up against them and fight for yourself. You are the most valuable thing in your life, and nobody or nothing is more important than yourself. Follow the above-mentioned steps and protect yourself from manipulators.

Conclusion

Thank you for making it through to the end of *Gaslighting Recovery*. Let's hope it was informative and able to provide you with all of the tools you need to achieve your goals, whatever they may be.

The next step is to start taking baby steps towards your recovery. The moment you take that first step, you are going to feel much more empowered because you know that you can no longer be controlled. It's important to remember that healing is a time-consuming process, and it is not going to happen overnight. So, if you don't see any quick results, you don't need to beat yourself up over it.

The internal strength that you will get with each step you take will push you more to do better. But you cannot give up. Surround yourself with people who truly want the best for you and want to see you transformed into the better version of yourself. The presence of such people around you will help in the process of healing and be a great emotional support.

With time, you will find yourself understanding your feelings and emotions better, and you will no longer feel anxious. This happens because you no longer keep your emotions buried – you feel them. Always keep in mind that there is nothing about emotional abuse that is your fault. Stop thinking that you made yourself vulnerable to the abuse – focus on how you are a powerful survivor who endured all of that and is now walking on the path of healing and self-compassion.

Finally, if you found this book useful in any way, a review on Amazon is always appreciated!